dailyinspirations

on

prayer

Carolyn Larsen

christian
art gifts®

Introduction

❧

Prayer is amazing. The very fact that we are invited, even commanded, to converse with Almighty God is nearly beyond comprehension. He loves us that much. And He wants us to love Him that much.

He cares about the things that we agonize over and the things we celebrate. We should never take the privilege of prayer lightly – even when we don't understand it. We can go to God, be alone with Him, tell Him what's on our hearts.

That's how we know Him more intimately. We can see Him working and moving in response to our prayers. Prayer is amazing.

Training Ground

Imagine you are about to run a triathlon (come on, just pretend). You know you have miles and miles ahead of you to run, swim and bike. It's going to be grueling. It's going to be tough. It's going to take every bit of your strength.

Of course, no sane person would go into this race without training for it. Working out trains your muscles to be able to endure the exertion of the race. The training is what makes it possible for you to finish the race.

Think of prayer as a training program. Prayer connects you to God and helps in the training of your faith muscles. As you tell God about the things you are concerned about and experience His comfort and peace, your faith muscle grows and that draws you closer to God.

The experience of prayer trains you to trust God more with the details of your life.

The LORD is near to all who call on Him, to all who call on Him in truth.

Psalm 145:18

God, who has called you into fellowship with His Son Jesus Christ our Lord, is faithful

1 Corinthians 1:9

If My people, who are called by My name, will humble themselves and pray and seek My face and turn from their wicked ways, then will I hear from heaven and will forgive their sin and will heal their land.

2 Chronicles 7:14

Know therefore that the LORD your God is God; He is the faithful God, keeping His covenant of love to a thousand generations of those who love Him and keep His commands.

Deuteronomy 7:9

For the eyes of the Lord are on the righteous and His ears are attentive to their prayer, but the face of the Lord is against those who do evil.

I Peter 3:12

I pray also that the eyes of your heart may be enlightened in order that you may know the hope to which He has called you, the riches of His glorious inheritance in the saints, and His incomparably great power for us who believe.

Ephesians 1:18-19

May my cry come before You, O LORD; give me understanding according to Your word.

Psalm 119:169

I guide you in the way of wisdom and lead you along straight paths.

Proverbs 4:11

Prayer is the gymnasium of the soul.
Samuel M. Zwemer

Dear Father, thank You for the training program of prayer. Sometimes it isn't easy to pray ... and wait for Your answer.

Help me to remember that my faith is being trained by the experiences of prayer. Give me the perseverance and diligence to stay in the program.

Amen.

Praise His Grace

So, your daughter is in the midst of parenting. She is dealing with strong-willed children who are experts at temper tantrums and battling bedtimes.

Nearly every day she calls you for advice and sympathy which you sincerely give. But when you hang up the phone, you smile. "There is justice," you think, "she's getting what she deserves." After all, when she was a toddler she put you through the wringer.

Maybe you think that's the way it should be – everyone should get what they deserve. Well, thank the good Lord we don't. If God allowed you to get what you deserve, there would be no possibility of heaven or even much of a relationship with Him. You'd be doomed to an eternity of punishment for your sin.

But by His amazing grace, you are forgiven. By His grace you can have a personal relationship with Him. By His grace you can look forward to eternity with Him. Praise God for His grace.

For the law was given through Moses; grace and truth came through Jesus Christ.

John 1:17

All have sinned and fall short of the glory of God, and are justified freely by His grace through the redemption that came by Christ Jesus.

Romans 3:23-24

Where sin increased, grace increased all the more, so that, just as sin reigned in death, so also grace might reign through righteousness to bring eternal life through Jesus Christ our Lord.

Romans 5:20-21

For it is by grace you have been saved, through faith – and this not from yourselves, it is the gift of God – not by works, so that no one can boast.

Ephesians 2:8-9

Let us then approach the throne of grace with confidence so that we may receive mercy and find grace to help us in our time of need.

Hebrews 4:16

Having been justified by His grace, we might become heirs having the hope of eternal life.

Titus 3:7

Be strong in the grace that is in Christ Jesus.

2 Timothy 2:1

May our Lord Jesus Christ Himself and God our Father, who loved us and by His grace gave us eternal encouragement and good hope, encourage your hearts and strengthen you in every good deed and word.

2 Thessalonians 2:16-17

God doesn't always smooth the path,
but sometimes He puts
springs in the wagon.

Marshall Lucas

❧

Dear Father, thank You for the "springs" – Your grace that makes the difficult times of life a little smoother – Your grace that forgives my sins and sets me on solid ground before You. Amen.

Adore His Wisdom

Trouble. Your car suddenly won't do what it's supposed to do – it won't run. Now, what if you had to lift the hood and figure out the problem on your own? Then what if you had to crawl beneath the car and fix the problem? Not a very appealing picture, is it?

When your car needs repairs you are quite thankful for the expertise of your trusted mechanic. You know he can fix the problem and you are so glad.

God's wisdom surpasses all other wisdom and it is available to you. Wisdom that is beyond your own yet is available to you, is a gift. God will guide you through questions you have about your future. He has the answers. He will give you wisdom in your struggles with decisions and choices.

All this divine wisdom is at your fingertips through the process of prayer. Scripture says that, "You don't have because you don't ask." God wants to share His wisdom with you ... just ask.

The fear of the LORD is the beginning of wisdom; all who follow His precepts have good understanding. To Him belongs eternal praise.

Psalm 111:10

God made the earth by His power; He founded the world by His wisdom and stretched out the heavens by His understanding.

Jeremiah 10:12

If any of you lacks wisdom, he should ask God, who gives generously to all without finding fault, and it will be given to him.

James 1:5

Oh, the depth of the riches of the wisdom and knowledge of God! How unsearchable His judgments, and His paths beyond tracing out!

Romans 11:33

"Call to Me and I will answer you and tell you great and unsearchable things you do not know."

Jeremiah 33:3

"For My thoughts are not your thoughts, neither are your ways My ways," declares the LORD. "As the heavens are higher than the earth, so are My ways higher than your ways and My thoughts than your thoughts."

Isaiah 55:8-9

"Ask and it will be given to you; seek and you will find; knock and the door will be opened to you. For everyone who asks receives; he who seeks finds; and to him who knocks, the door will be opened."

Matthew 7:7-8

My son, if you accept my words and store up my commands within you, turning your ear to wisdom and applying your heart to understanding, and if you call out for insight and cry aloud for understanding, and if you look for it as for silver and search for it as for hidden treasure, then you will understand the fear of the LORD and find the knowledge of God.

Proverbs 2:1-5

Wisdom is the power to see and the inclination to choose the best and highest goal, together with the surest means of attaining it.

J. I. Packer

Dear Father, wisdom is what I need ... Your wisdom to guide my choices, my actions and my words. Father, please give me Your wisdom and the strength to follow it.

Amen.

Confessing
Self-Centeredness

Of course you care about other people. What kind of selfish person wouldn't care about others? You may be saying the right words to show your concern for others. You may be doing the right things. But your concern for others is restricted to what is convenient for you and your comfort zones. Basically, deep down inside, your greatest concern is for ... yourself.

There is a constant pull to focus on yourself and how life affects you. Relationships that are for your benefit become the most important. You seek out situations that make you look good. You can hide these kinds of feelings from other people – cover them up so no one suspects. But you can't hide them from God.

His command to you is to love others and self-centeredness is a real block to that love. It's necessary to admit your feelings, confess them and repent.

Love is patient, love is kind. It does not envy, it does not boast, it is not proud. It is not self-seeking, it is not easily angered, it keeps no record of wrongs.

I Corinthians 13:4-5

"Do not seek revenge or bear a grudge against one of your people, but love your neighbor as yourself. I am the Lord."

Leviticus 19:18

Your love, O Lord, reaches to the heavens, Your faithfulness to the skies.

Psalm 36:5

If we confess our sins, He is faithful and just and will forgive us our sins and purify us from all unrighteousness.

I John 1:9

Let us then approach the throne of grace with confidence, so that we may receive mercy and find grace to help us in our time of need.

Hebrews 4:16

You hear, O LORD, the desire of the afflicted; You encourage them, and You listen to their cry.

Psalm 10:17

Love your neighbor as yourself. Love does no harm to its neighbor. Therefore love is the fulfillment of the law.

Romans 13:9-10

"Greater love has no one than this, that he lay down his life for his friends."

John 15:13

Be not proud of race,
face, place or grace.
Charles H. Spurgeon

Dear Father, this one hurts – sometimes I'm so consumed with ... me. Forgive me, Father, for trying to take credit for what You've done and what You've given me. Father, forgive me for carrying pride out in front of me.
Amen.

Thanksgiving

It's a good thing to get into the habit of saying thank you. You've probably taught your children to write thank you notes.

Perhaps you've tried to set a good example for them and you're pretty good at remembering to say thanks yourself. You thank those who serve you and those who help you. You gratefully thank those who give you gifts. But, do you remember the most important thank You of all?

There is so much to be thankful for and it all comes from God. In fact, He is so generous and giving that it becomes easy to just expect all He gives.

There is a daily danger of taking God's many gifts for granted and forgetting to thank Him for some of the things that mean the most to you – friends, family, your church, your health – all gifts from God's gracious hand.

Give thanks to the LORD, for He is good; His love endures forever.

I Chronicles 16:34

Enter His gates with thanksgiving and His courts with praise; give thanks to Him and praise His name. For the LORD is good and His love endures forever.

Psalm 100:4-5

Thanks be to God, who always leads us in triumphal procession in Christ and through us spreads everywhere the fragrance of the knowledge of Him.

2 Corinthians 2:14

Be joyful always; pray continually; give thanks in all circumstances, for this is God's will for you in Christ Jesus.

I Thessalonians 5:16-18

Let us come before Him with thanksgiving and extol Him with music and song.

Psalm 95:2

Every good and perfect gift is from above, coming down from the Father of the heavenly lights, who does not change like shifting shadows.

James 1:17

The LORD will indeed give what is good, and our land will yield its harvest.

Psalm 85:12

For the wages of sin is death, but the gift of God is eternal life in Christ Jesus our Lord.

Romans 6:23

The failure to return thanks for definite blessings received is a manifestation of ingratitude that grieves Jesus Christ.

R. A. Torrey

Dear Father, do I really forget to thank You for all You've done for me and given me? Please, do not let me ever take things for granted.

Father, remind me daily that all I have, all I will ever have, and all that I am, are because of You and Your love for me.

Amen.

Help, Please!

Have you ever felt this way? You can't concentrate on anything. There's a knot in the pit of your stomach. You can't sleep. You can't relax, your muscles are tensed all the time. What's causing this physical condition? Worry.

Someone you love very much is very sick. The doctors have decreed that they have done all they can and now the very life of this loved one is in the best place possible – God's hands.

What can you do? Pray. Pray with all your heart for God's healing hand to be on your loved one. Ask God to encourage and sustain with His power and His peace.

Sometimes it feels that there's nothing you can do for a sick loved one, but that's never true. You can petition the power of the God of the universe on behalf of your loved one who needs His healing power.

Dear friend, I pray that you may enjoy good health and that all may go well with you, even as your soul is getting along well.

3 John 2

Jesus went through all the towns and villages, teaching in their synagogues, preaching the good news of the kingdom and healing every disease and sickness.

Matthew 9:35

Praise the LORD, O my soul, and forget not all His benefits – who forgives all your sins and heals all your diseases.

Psalm 103:2-3

He sent forth His word and healed them; He rescued them from the grave.

Psalm 107:20

Heal me, O LORD, and I will be healed; save me and I will be saved, for You are the one I praise.

Jeremiah 17:14

Is any one of you sick? He should call the elders of the church to pray over him and anoint him with oil in the name of the Lord. And the prayer offered in faith will make the sick person well; the Lord will raise him up. If he has sinned, he will be forgiven.

James 5:14-15

My son, pay attention to what I say; listen closely to my words. Do not let them out of your sight, keep them within your heart; for they are life to those who find them and health to a man's whole body.

Proverbs 4:20-22

The centurion replied, "Lord, I do not deserve to have You come under my roof. But just say the word, and my servant will be healed."

Matthew 8:8

Prayer is not overcoming God's reluctance, but laying hold of His willingness.
Martin Luther

Dear Father, do You understand that feeling we get when someone we love is ill? Really ill? O God, I cry out to You to heal my loved one, restore her to complete health.

Thank You for hearing my prayer, for caring and loving. Father, thank You that I can trust You completely.

Amen.

Praise for Love

There is nothing more important to God than love. That sounds so basic, doesn't it? The fact is that He's the Author of love itself. However, His unconditional love is truly beyond human comprehension.

The greatest commandment given to us, according to God's Word, is to love God and love others. When we love we are most like God. Unfortunately it's not always easy for us to love because we get focused on how things affect us and our viewpoint gets twisted to think we are more important than anyone else.

But God's love is so pure and honest that it forgives even the most horrible things. God loves even when that love isn't returned. He loves even when the objects of His love disappoint Him. God's love is constant and forgiving. God's love is the model for us. It gives us a goal to reach for. Praise God for His love.

Dear friends, let us love one another, for love comes from God. Everyone who loves has been born of God and knows God. Whoever does not love does not know God, because God is love.

1 John 4:7-8

"A new command I give you: Love one another. As I have loved you, so you must love one another. By this all men will know that you are My disciples, if you love one another."

John 13:34-35

"I have loved you with an everlasting love; I have drawn you with loving-kindness."

Jeremiah 31:3

If anyone obeys His word, God's love is truly made complete in him.

1 John 2:5

"The most important [commandment]," answered Jesus, "is this: 'Love the Lord your God with all your heart and with all your soul and with all your mind and with all your strength.' The second is this: 'Love your neighbor as yourself.' There is no commandment greater than these."

Mark 12:29-31

All the ways of the LORD are loving and faithful for those who keep the demands of His covenant.

Psalm 25:10

Love must be sincere.

Romans 12:9

Do everything in love.

1 Corinthians 16:14

Love is an act of endless forgiveness.
                                        Jean Vanier

Dear Father, thank You for loving me so completely. I trust that Your love is pure and honest with no grudges held. You love me. Help me to love You completely, and to model Your love to others.

                                        Amen.

Fake Front

Have you ever known someone who appeared to have life under control? A person who seemed to have every aspect of life together?

She's the Proverbs 31 woman and more – squeaky clean house, gourmet cook, home decorator beyond compare, always a candidate for Mother of the Year ... ? You get the idea. She makes you feel like you have a perpetual bad hair day. Well, more than likely she's got some issues that she keeps hidden from the world. Most people do.

You can put up a good front to the world. You can appear to have everything together and hide the areas where you're failing. You can even try to do that with God.

But the truth is ... and you know it ... that you're not fooling Him. It's so much better to just admit your failures to God and stop trying to fool Him. Confess, repent and be honest with God.

I confess my iniquity; I am troubled by my sin.

Psalm 38:18

If you confess with your mouth, "Jesus is Lord," and believe in your heart that God raised Him from the dead, you will be saved.

Romans 10:9

At the name of Jesus every knee should bow, in heaven and on earth and under the earth, and every tongue confess that Jesus Christ is Lord, to the glory of God the Father.

Philippians 2:10-11

Make confession to the LORD, the God of your fathers, and do His will.

Ezra 10:11

He who conceals his sins does not prosper, but whoever confesses and renounces them finds mercy.

Proverbs 28:13

Then I acknowledged my sin to You and did not cover up my iniquity. I said, "I will confess my transgressions to the LORD" – and You forgave the guilt of my sin.

Psalm 32:5

Who may ascend the hill of the LORD? Who may stand in His holy place? He who has clean hands and a pure heart, who does not lift up his soul to an idol or swear by what is false.

Psalm 24:3-4

Holding on to faith and a good conscience. Some have rejected these and so have shipwrecked their faith.

I Timothy 1:19

*God can never entrust His Kingdom
to anyone who has not been
broken of pride, for pride
is the armor of darkness itself.*

Francis Frangipane

Dear Father, I know that sometimes I think
too highly of myself. I'm sorry for that pride.
Father, help me to think of others more highly
than myself. Help me to push others in front
and be willing to stand in the background.

Amen.

Thanks for Family

Family – the people who know the real you. You can absolutely be yourself with your family. You don't have to put up any pretenses and your family will love you and forgive you for your shortcomings.

Family ends up being the people you love the most but who can make you the most crazy. Living together in close quarters can bring out the best and worst of people. However, God knows that families are important. He even uses the family analogy to describe His relationship with us. He created families to begin with.

The family relationship is the closest. You share memories of your entire life with your siblings. Stories of childhood holidays, quirky relatives, and trips to Grandma's house are only shared with family.

Your biggest cheerleaders, strongest advocates, and energetic protectors are your family. Thank God for your family.

Train up a child in the way he should go, and when he is old he will not turn from it.

Proverbs 22:6

Finally, all of you, live in harmony with one another; be sympathetic, love as brothers, be compassionate and humble. Do not repay evil with evil or insult with insult, but with blessing, because to this you were called so that you may inherit a blessing.

I Peter 3:8-9

He and all his family were devout and God-fearing; he gave generously to those in need and prayed to God regularly.

Acts 10:2

Respect those who work hard among you, who are over you in the Lord and who admonish you. Hold them in the highest regard in love because of their work. Live in peace with each other.

I Thessalonians 5:12-13

Be devoted to one another in brotherly love. Honor one another above yourselves.

Romans 12:10

Better a dry crust with peace and quiet than a house full of feasting, with strife.

Proverbs 17:1

A wife of noble character who can find? She is worth far more than rubies. Her husband has full confidence in her and lacks nothing of value.

Proverbs 31:10-11

She watches over the affairs of her household and does not eat the bread of idleness. Her children arise and call her blessed; her husband also, and he praises her: "Many women do noble things, but you surpass them all."

Proverbs 31:27-29

Call it a clan, call it a network, call it a tribe, call it a family. Whatever you call it, whoever you are, you need one.
Jane Howard

❧

Dear Father, sometimes my family makes me crazy, but even in those times, I'm thankful for them. I love each one of them and I know they love me. I know I can count on them no matter what happens. Thank You for my family.
Amen.

The Scary World

So much of the news from around the world is just downright frightening. It's filled with the most horrific things that people do to other people.

In some parts of the world people must live in situations where they are in constant danger. Just being able to make it from day to day in safety and provide food for their children takes all their energy.

The political leaders of our world have a massive job of attempting to set peace among nations, bridge differences between political groups, tribes, religions and those with different priorities. It's incredible.

Political leaders need your prayers more today than at any time in history. Bring them to God and ask for wisdom and discernment and for them to seek to honor God in their decisions.

Bring world religious leaders to Him, too. Ask God to guide these men and women to be examples of His love. Our world leaders need God more than ever.

Remember your leaders, who spoke the word of God to you. Consider the outcome of their way of life and imitate their faith. Jesus Christ is the same yesterday and today and forever.

Hebrews 13:7-8

This is my prayer: that your love may abound more and more in knowledge and depth of insight, so that you may be able to discern what is best and may be pure and blameless until the day of Christ, filled with the fruit of righteousness that comes through Jesus Christ – to the glory and praise of God.

Philippians 1:9-11

This is the confidence we have in approaching God: that if we ask anything according to His will, He hears us. And if we know that He hears us – whatever we ask – we know that we have what we asked of Him.

1 John 5:14-15

The discerning heart seeks knowledge, but the mouth of a fool feeds on folly.

Proverbs 15:14

The fear of the LORD is the beginning of wisdom; all who follow His precepts have good understanding. To Him belongs eternal praise.

Psalm 111:10

Obey your leaders and submit to their authority. They keep watch over you as men who must give an account. Obey them so that their work will be a joy, not a burden, for that would be of no advantage to you.

Hebrews 13:17

For the foolishness of God is wiser than man's wisdom, and the weakness of God is stronger than man's strength.

1 Corinthians 1:25

Everyone must submit himself to the governing authorities, for there is no authority except that which God has established. The authorities that exist have been established by God.

Romans 13:1

God has wisely kept us in the dark
concerning future events and reserved
for Himself the knowledge of them
that He may train us up in a
dependence upon Himself and a
continued readiness for every event.

Matthew Henry

❧

Dear Father, our world is a scary place these days. I do pray for leaders around the world. Father, I pray that these men and women would listen to You, seek to honor and follow You. Father, give them wisdom and guide them to work together.

Amen.

His Constant Presence

Are you courageous? It's easier to be brave when you've got your team around you than it is when you're completely alone, isn't it?

Your team may be your family, friends, or co-workers with similar passions and goals. When you're working with others you have a support group to encourage you and to motivate you. But when you're alone, you're, well, alone.

Thank God that you are never alone. Scripture is filled with God's promise to be with you always. There will be times when you can't "feel" His presence, but you can trust His word that He is always with you, in good times and bad. There will be times in life when you can look back at a harrowing experience and see His hand of protection and guidance.

Those times will give you confidence for the next time you need to be assured of His presence. Praise God for His presence.

"You will seek Me and find Me when you seek Me with all your heart. I will be found by you," declares the LORD.

Jeremiah 29:13-14

Where can I go from Your Spirit? Where can I flee from Your presence? If I go up to the heavens, You are there; if I make my bed in the depths, You are there. If I rise on the wings of the dawn, if I settle on the far side of the sea, even there Your hand will guide me, Your right hand will hold me fast.

Psalm 139:7-10

Come near to God and He will come near to you.

James 4:8

My flesh and my heart may fail, but God is the strength of my heart and my portion forever.

Psalm 73:26

"Where two or three come together in My name, there am I with them."

Matthew 18:20

This is the covenant I will make with the house of Israel after that time, declares the Lord. I will put My laws in their minds and write them on their hearts. I will be their God, and they will be My people.

Hebrews 8:10

"So do not fear, for I am with you; do not be dismayed, for I am your God. I will strengthen you and help you; I will uphold you with My righteous right hand."

Isaiah 41:10

Neither height nor depth, nor anything else in all creation, will be able to separate us from the love of God that is in Christ Jesus our Lord.

Romans 8:39

Few delights can equal the mere presence of One whom we fully trust.
George McDonald

Dear Father, the knowledge that You are always with me is what keeps me going sometimes. Thank You that I am never alone – and that I will never face anything without You.

Amen.

God's Plan

There is no denying that life is busy. In our mobile, high-tech world there are no shortages of ways to spend your time.

In fact, it's a challenge to set priorities and stick to them. Many things that cry out for your time and energy are good things that need to be done. However, they may not be things that *you* need to do.

God has a plan for your life. All you have to do is talk to Him about what that plan is. He wants to tell you, but sometimes the path to finding that plan requires some work. Perhaps God wants to know you're serious about knowing Him so He asks you to make an effort to learn His plan.

That's where prayer comes in, ask God for direction and guidance in discovering His will for your life. Praise God for His plan.

Trust in the Lord with all your heart and lean not on your own understanding; in all your ways acknowledge Him, and He will make your paths straight.

Proverbs 3:5-6

"I will instruct you and teach you in the way you should go; I will counsel you and watch over you."

Psalm 32:8

"For I know the plans I have for you," declares the Lord, "plans to prosper you and not to harm you, plans to give you hope and a future."

Jeremiah 29:11

Many, O Lord my God, are the wonders You have done. The things You planned for us no one can recount to You; were I to speak and tell of them, they would be too many to declare.

Psalm 40:5

Humble yourselves before the Lord, and He will lift you up.

James 4:10

This is the confidence we have in approaching God: that if we ask anything according to His will, He hears us. And if we know that He hears us – whatever we ask – we know that we have what we asked of Him.

I John 5:14-15

In Him we were also chosen, having been predestined according to the plan of Him who works out everything in conformity with the purpose of His will, in order that we, who were the first to hope in Christ, might be for the praise of His glory.

Ephesians 1:11-12

Commit to the LORD whatever you do, and your plans will succeed.

Proverbs 16:3

The beautiful thing about this adventure called faith is that we can count on Him never to lead us astray.
Chuck Swindoll

Dear Father, thank You for having a plan for my life. Sometimes I can't see it and I don't know which way to turn. But I know if I just stop and listen for Your guidance, it will be there.

Amen.

Timely Confession

What happens when you are reunited with a good friend you haven't seen for a long time? Do you say a quick hello and then go on your way? Probably not.

More than likely you settle down with a cup of hot cocoa and talk late into the night. Spending time with a dear friend is a real joy. You want to hear all that's going on in her life and share what is happening in yours.

Do you place this same kind of importance on your relationship with God? He desires to know you and for you to know Him. He waits every day for you to spend time with Him; read His Word; talk with Him and listen for Him to speak with you.

How often does the busyness of life infringe on your time with God? You won't grow closer to God just because you have good intentions. Confess that you don't spend regular time communing with God and ask for strength to make time with God a daily joy.

Grow in the grace and knowledge of our Lord and Savior Jesus Christ. To Him be glory both now and forever!

2 Peter 3:18

Like newborn babies, crave pure spiritual milk, so that by it you may grow up in your salvation, now that you have tasted that the Lord is good.

1 Peter 2:2-3

Taste and see that the Lord is good; blessed is the man who takes refuge in Him.

Psalm 34:8

Then I acknowledged my sin to You and did not cover up my iniquity. I said, "I will confess my transgressions to the Lord" – and You forgave the guilt of my sin.

Psalm 32:5

"Be still, and know that I am God; I will be exalted among the nations, I will be exalted in the earth."

Psalm 46:10

Be still before the LORD, all mankind, because He has roused Himself from His holy dwelling.

Zechariah 2:13

Humble yourselves before the Lord, and He will lift you up.

James 4:10

Do your best to present yourself to God as one approved, a workman who does not need to be ashamed and who correctly handles the word of truth.

2 Timothy 2:15

*It is impossible for a man
to be freed from the habit of sin
before he hates it, just as it is
impossible to receive forgiveness
before confessing his trespasses.*

Ignatius

❧

Dear Father, I'm sorry that I ignore the need for confession so often. I guess I think that my sins aren't real if I don't say them out loud. Please forgive me for that.

Father, help me take the time and make the effort to come clean with You. I trust You to forgive me.

Amen.

Thanks for Laughter

Laughter is like sunshine on a dark, cold, dreary day. Regardless of what is going on in your life, sharing laughter with a friend is a respite from reality.

It gives a moment of hope that things will get better and that there is still joy in the universe. It isn't much fun to laugh alone. Hearty-deep-from-inside laughter connects you with another person. There will be times in the future when you look back at that moment of joyous hilarity and share a memory about it.

Thank God for laughter. He knew how important laughter would be for His children – look around at some of the things He created and you can almost imagine His joyous laughter.

Thank Him for the reminder that however hard life is today, it will be better in the future. Let yourself laugh. Share laughter with others.

[There is] a time to weep and a time to laugh.

Ecclesiastes 3:4

A happy heart makes the face cheerful, but heart-ache crushes the spirit.

Proverbs 15:13

A cheerful heart is good medicine, but a crushed spirit dries up the bones.

Proverbs 17:22

Nehemiah said, "Go and enjoy choice food and sweet drinks, and send some to those who have nothing prepared. This day is sacred to our Lord. Do not grieve, for the joy of the Lord is your strength."

Nehemiah 8:10

Surely You have granted him eternal blessings and made him glad with the joy of Your presence.

Psalm 21:6

"I have told you this so that My joy may be in you and that your joy may be complete."

John 15:11

The angel said to them, "Do not be afraid. I bring you good news of great joy that will be for all the people."

Luke 2:10

Is any one of you in trouble? He should pray. Is anyone happy? Let him sing songs of praise.

James 5:13

Shared laughter creates a bond of friendship. When people laugh together, they cease to be young and old, master and pupils, worker and driver.
They have become a single group of human beings, enjoying their existence.

W. Grant Lee

❧

Dear Father, thank You for laughter. A really good laugh is cleansing and gives the energy and strength to keep on going. Thanks for knowing that we would need to laugh.

Amen.

The Parents' Prayer

Life can be stressful when your children are young. As a dedicated mother, you want to be careful to teach them the things they will need to become mature adults. More than anything, you want to protect your children throughout their childhood.

You are careful to keep them close by when out shopping. You watch them closely at the park. You teach them to be careful about speaking with strangers. However, as your children grow into teenagers, you may realize that much of your teaching is done. The groundwork is laid. Have you taught them what they need? Will they make good choices? Will they seek God's direction?

It is always important to pray for your children. However, it becomes more and more important as they grow into adulthood and begin making choices which will impact their future. Ask God to protect them from the danger of impulse bad choices.

It's a privilege to bring your children before God and invoke His blessing and guidance on their lives.

Even a child is known by his actions, by whether his conduct is pure and right.

Proverbs 20:11

Impress the [commandments] on your children. Talk about them when you sit at home and when you walk along the road, when you lie down and when you get up. Tie them as symbols on your hands and bind them on your foreheads. Write them on the doorframes of your houses and on your gates.

Deuteronomy 6:7-9

Do not exasperate your children; instead, bring them up in the training and instruction of the Lord.

Ephesians 6:4

He will turn the hearts of the fathers to their children, and the hearts of the children to their fathers; or else I will come and strike the land with a curse.

Malachi 4:6

In the morning, O LORD, You hear my voice; in the morning I lay my requests before You and wait in expectation.

Psalm 5:3

Sons are a heritage from the LORD, children a reward from Him. Like arrows in the hands of a warrior are sons born in one's youth. Blessed is the man whose quiver is full of them.

Psalm 127:3-5

Children's children are a crown to the aged, and parents are the pride of their children.

Proverbs 17:6

All your sons will be taught by the LORD, and great will be your children's peace.

Isaiah 54:13

The father of a righteous man has great joy; he who has a wise son delights in him.

Proverbs 23:24

Pray, and let God worry.
Martin Luther

Dear Father, I pray that each of my children will become Christ-followers. I pray that they will turn to You. I love my children dearly. Please guide and protect them.

Amen.

Thank God for His Mercy

Mercy is when you don't get what you deserve. Perhaps you can identify with the joy that mercy brings. Have you ever been stopped for speeding? A knot develops in the pit of your stomach as you see the policeman walking toward your car. You know that you were indeed speeding, but still you feel ... caught. You politely give him your insurance information and glumly wait for the ticket to be written. However, when he comes back and says he is just giving you a warning, relief flows through your being and you energetically promise that you will NEVER drive over the speed limit again. Mercy has been shown.

It's funny that we can get so excited about speeding ticket mercies and yet not truly grasp the mercy that God shows us. Based on our sinfulness and deliberate disobedience, we deserve nothing from God.

Yet He allows us a personal relationship with Him, He provides the sacrifice for our sins, and He will permit us eternity with Him. Mercy. Praise God for mercy.

The LORD your God is a merciful God; He will not abandon or destroy you or forget the covenant with your forefathers, which He confirmed to them by oath.

Deuteronomy 4:31

You warned them to return to Your law, but they became arrogant and disobeyed Your commands. They sinned against Your ordinances, by which a man will live if he obeys them ... But in Your great mercy You did not put an end to them or abandon them, for You are a gracious and merciful God.

Nehemiah 9:29-31

"Blessed are the merciful, for they will be shown mercy."

Matthew 5:7

He had to be made like his brothers in every way, in order that he might become a merciful and faithful high priest in service to God, and that he might make atonement for the sins of the people.

Hebrews 2:17

In all their distress He too was distressed, and the angel of His presence saved them. In His love and mercy He redeemed them; He lifted them up and carried them all the days of old.

Isaiah 63:9

Praise be to the God and Father of our Lord Jesus Christ! In His great mercy He has given us new birth into a living hope through the resurrection of Jesus Christ from the dead, and into an inheritance that can never perish, spoil or fade – kept in heaven for you, who through faith are shielded by God's power until the coming of the salvation that is ready to be revealed in the last time.

I Peter 1:3-5

Speak and act as those who are going to be judged by the law that gives freedom, because judgment without mercy will be shown to anyone who has not been merciful. Mercy triumphs over judgment!

James 2:12-13

God forgave us without
any merit on our part, therefore,
we must forgive others, whether
or not we think they merit it.

Lehman Strauss

Dear Father, I'm so thankful for Your mercy.
Thank You for not giving me what I deserve.

Amen.

Confessing Feelings of Hatred

There's an old saying which says, "There is a thin line between love and hate." That's because both are powerfully strong emotions.

Hopefully you've not ever truly felt hatred because when you feel strong negative emotions toward another person it's impossible to wish any good will toward them.

It's bad enough to have such bad feelings toward another person, but these ill feelings are also a direct disobedience to God's command to love one another.

Oh sure, some people are difficult to love and some people deliberately do things to hurt others. But the bottom line is that you aren't responsible for their actions and do not have to answer to God for them. You are responsible only for yourself.

So, if you find strong feelings of dislike, bordering on hatred, taking up residence in your heart, the best thing is to confess it to God and ask His help in getting beyond those feelings. He will help if you let Him. Just ask.

Hatred stirs up dissension, but love covers over all wrongs.

Proverbs 10:12

He who covers over an offense promotes love, but whoever repeats the matter separates close friends.

Proverbs 17:9

Love is patient, love is kind. It does not envy, it does not boast, it is not proud. It is not rude, it is not self-seeking, it is not easily angered, it keeps no record of wrongs. Love does not delight in evil but rejoices with the truth. It always protects, always trusts, always hopes, always perseveres.

1 Corinthians 13:4-7

"You have heard that it was said, 'Love your neighbor and hate your enemy.' But I tell you: Love your enemies and pray for those who persecute you, that you may be sons of your Father in heaven. He causes His sun to rise on the evil and the good, and sends rain on the righteous and the unrighteous."

Matthew 5:43-45

Above all, love each other deeply, because love covers over a multitude of sins.

I Peter 4:8

Bless those who persecute you; bless and do not curse. Do not repay anyone evil for evil. Be careful to do what is right in the eyes of everybody. If it is possible, as far as it depends on you, live at peace with everyone.

Romans 12:14, 17-18

"If your enemy is hungry, feed him; if he is thirsty, give him something to drink. In doing this, you will heap burning coals on his head." Do not be overcome by evil, but overcome evil with good.

Romans 12:20-21

Search me, O God, and know my heart; test me and know my anxious thoughts. See if there is any offensive way in me, and lead me in the way ever-lasting.

Psalm 139:23-24

There are few things as pathetic
and terrible to behold as
the person who has harbored
a grudge, or hatred, over the years.
David Johnson

Dear Father, please help me overcome these
negative feelings. Help me to love those who
hurt and anger me. Father, love through me.
Amen.

Thanks for Friends

Good friends are like the sunlight of life. Sharing life, both happy times and difficult times, with friends enriches life. Friends can encourage you to be the person God intends for you to be.

Your friends should lift you up and motivate you to grow and mature. True friends will listen to you spill your inmost feelings and keep that information buried, never sharing a drop of it with others. Your secrets are safe with them. Friends listen to you vent about family members or co-workers, then promptly forget the vented feelings so their own opinions of those people are not colored. Friends dream with you and hold you accountable to goals you've set.

Friends are like strong handrails that guide you as you cross over some of the canyons of life. They support you, protect you, hold you in line. Thank God for friends. They are truly a gift from God.

A friend loves at all times, and a brother is born for adversity.

Proverbs 17:17

Blessed is the man who does not walk in the counsel of the wicked or stand in the way of sinners or sit in the seat of mockers.

Psalm 1:1

Wounds from a friend can be trusted, but an enemy multiplies kisses.

Proverbs 27:6

Select capable men from all the people – men who fear God, trustworthy men who hate dishonest gain – and appoint them as officials over thousands, hundreds, fifties and tens. That will make your load lighter, because they will share it with you.

Exodus 18:21-22

Two are better than one, because they have a good return for their work: If one falls down, his friend can help him up. But pity the man who falls and has no one to help him up!

Ecclesiastes 4:9-10

Each one should use whatever gift he has received to serve others, faithfully administering God's grace in its various forms.

1 Peter 4:10

An unfriendly man pursues selfish ends; he defies all sound judgment.

Proverbs 18:1

The heart of the discerning acquires knowledge; the ears of the wise seek it out.

Proverbs 18:15

Friendship is one of the sweetest joys of life. Many might have failed beneath the bitterness of their trial had they not found a friend.

Charles H. Spurgeon

Dear Father, I'm so thankful for my friends. They truly make my life more enjoyable. They support me in hard times and celebrate in good ones.

Amen.

For Salvation

The Christians in developing countries seem to really "get it." They generally seem to have a better handle on the urgency of sharing the gospel with the lost.

Time is running short and God desires that all people have a chance to hear and choose for themselves whether or not to follow Him. Many of these believers not only pray for the salvation of loved ones but they do what they must do to bring the message of God's love to the attention of people.

Unfortunately too many Christians are lukewarm about the importance of sharing Christ – for which they will answer to God. Look around you at family, friends, co-workers who do not know Christ.

Think about entire groups of people who have not yet had a chance to hear. Ask God to give you a passion to pray for the salvation of these people, both those you know and those you won't know until heaven.

We are therefore Christ's ambassadors, as though God were making His appeal through us.

2 Corinthians 5:20

"If a man owns a hundred sheep, and one of them wanders away, will he not leave the ninety-nine on the hills and go to look for the one that wandered off? And if he finds it, I tell you the truth, he is happier about that one sheep than about the ninety-nine that did not wander off. In the same way your Father in heaven is not willing that any of these little ones should be lost."

Matthew 18:12-14

Live such good lives among the pagans that, though they accuse you of doing wrong, they may see your good deeds and glorify God on the day He visits us.

1 Peter 2:12

The Lord is not slow in keeping His promise, as some understand slowness. He is patient with you, not wanting anyone to perish, but everyone to come to repentance.

2 Peter 3:9

"Therefore go and make disciples of all nations, baptizing them in the name of the Father and of the Son and of the Holy Spirit, and teaching them to obey everything I have commanded you. And surely I am with you always, to the very end of the age."

Matthew 28:19-20

Those who are wise will shine like the brightness of the heavens, and those who lead many to righteousness, like the stars for ever and ever.

Daniel 12:3

"Come, follow Me," Jesus said, "and I will make you fishers of men."

Mark 1:17

"Not everyone who says to Me, 'Lord, Lord,' will enter the kingdom of heaven, but only he who does the will of My Father who is in heaven. Many will say to Me on that day, "Lord, Lord, did we not prophesy in Your name, and in Your name drive out demons and perform many miracles?' Then I will tell them plainly, 'I never knew you. Away from Me, you evildoers!'"

Matthew 7:21-23

*The Blood of Jesus washes
away our past and the name
of Jesus opens up our future.*

Jesse Duplantis

*Dear Father, thank You for saving me. I know
my salvation did not come free to You – it
cost You something. Thank You for loving me
that much.*

Amen.

Praise God's Unchangeableness

For so many women, moods are the air in which we live and breathe. Our good moods and bad moods float in and around us, coloring relationships, attitudes and choices. Our children never know if they will walk in to find "Happy, Loving Mom" or "Psycho Mom."

It's not a fun way to live. Perhaps you are more even-tempered, but, more than likely, someone in your world is a moody person. It can be so difficult to deal with a person like this. You find yourself walking on eggshells around her so you don't upset her or arouse her temper.

This kind of person makes God's unchanging character even more precious. He is the same every day, every hour, every minute. God is love. God is righteous. God is merciful. God is grace. His character never changes and He does not act or move apart from who He is.

Moods play no part in who God is. Praise God for His unchanging characteristics and attributes.

"Therefore everyone who hears these words of Mine and puts them into practice is like a wise man who built his house on the rock. The rain came down, the streams rose, and the winds blew and beat against that house; yet it did not fall, because it had its foundation on the rock."

Matthew 7:24-25

I waited patiently for the LORD; He turned to me and heard my cry. He lifted me out of the slimy pit, out of the mud and mire; He set my feet on a rock and gave me a firm place to stand.

Psalm 40:1-2

Do not be anxious about anything, but in everything, by prayer and petition, with thanksgiving, present your requests to God. And the peace of God, which transcends all understanding, will guard your hearts and your minds in Christ Jesus.

Philippians 4:6-7

Jesus Christ is the same yesterday and today and forever.

Hebrews 13:8

You remain the same, and Your years will never end.

Psalm 102:27

Every good and perfect gift is from above, coming down from the Father of the heavenly lights, who does not change like shifting shadows.

James 1:17

The LORD reigns forever; He has established His throne for judgment.

Psalm 9:7

"I the LORD do not change. So you, O descendants of Jacob, are not destroyed."

Malachi 3:6

God is not greater if you reverence Him, but you are greater if you serve Him.

St. Augustine

Dear Father, there aren't many things in this life that I can count on. You are the only thing I can think of. Thank You for always being there for me. Thank You that I can count on Your love, guidance and forgiveness.

Amen.

Too Much of Everything

There is an unbalance in this world. Some people have so very much in the way of material goods and safe places to live. Others have so very little – not enough food or water, no safe place to live. It's not fair.

Does an awareness of this unbalance change anything about the way you live? Or are you guilty of over-consumption? Scripture calls it gluttony – eating more than you need, using more than you need, even wasting what you don't use. Go all the way back to the story of God's provision of manna for the Israelites. His instruction was, "Each day take all you need; but only what you need. Don't try to hoard the manna."

No one may know of your gluttony ... except you and God. But, you and God are the only ones who need to know. Confess this sin to Him. Ask for His help in controlling it and for opportunities to share what you have with those who have needs.

"Bring the whole tithe into the storehouse, that there may be food in My house. Test Me in this," says the LORD Almighty, "and see if I will not throw open the floodgates of heaven and pour out so much blessing that you will not have room enough for it."

Malachi 3:10

Jesus saw the rich putting their gifts into the temple treasury. He also saw a poor widow put in two very small copper coins. "I tell you the truth," He said, "this poor widow has put in more than all the others. All these people gave their gifts out of their wealth; but she out of her poverty put in all she had to live on."

Luke 21:1-4

Everything comes from You, and we have given You only what comes from Your hand.

1 Chronicles 29:14

He who gives to the poor will lack nothing, but he who closes his eyes to them receives many curses.

Proverbs 28:27

"If anyone gives even a cup of cold water to one of these little ones because he is My disciple, I tell you the truth, he will certainly not lose his reward."

Matthew 10:42

"Give, and it will be given to you. A good measure, pressed down, shaken together and running over, will be poured into your lap. For with the measure you use, it will be measured to you."

Luke 6:38

In everything I did, I showed you that by this kind of hard work we must help the weak, remembering the words the Lord Jesus Himself said: "It is more blessed to give than to receive."

Acts 20:35

If you spend yourselves in behalf of the hungry and satisfy the needs of the oppressed, then your light will rise in the darkness, and your night will become like the noonday.

Isaiah 58:10

*Glutton: one who digs
his grave with his teeth.*

French Proverb

❧

*Dear Father, it's too easy to dismiss the un-
balance in the world when my life is so com-
fortable. Father, keep it before my mind that
I need ... must ... share what You have blessed
me with.*

Amen.

Praise God for His Word

There is so much to be thankful for. It must please God when some of your prayers are consumed with thanks instead of requests. That shows an awareness of all He does for you and gives you every day.

One thing to remember to thank God for is His Word. What a wonderful gift the Bible is. God cared that His children would be able to understand how Jesus related to people while He walked on earth. Scriptures record His teaching and His challenges. They give you a model of how He lived. Scripture also reveals God's character as you read how He interacted with His people, met their needs and judged them.

God expects loving obedience from His children. The Scriptures tell you how to live in obedience. The Bible is alive with His guidance. Reading it changes who you are. Thank God for His Word.

All Scripture is God-breathed and is useful for teaching, rebuking, correcting and training in righteousness, so that the man of God may be thoroughly equipped for every good work.

2 Timothy 3:16-17

Above all, you must understand that no prophecy of Scripture came about by the prophet's own interpretation. For prophecy never had its origin in the will of man, but men spoke from God as they were carried along by the Holy Spirit.

2 Peter 1:20-21

Your word is a lamp to my feet and a light for my path.

Psalm 119:105

I have not departed from the commands of His lips; I have treasured the words of His mouth more than my daily bread.

Job 23:12

Do not let this Book of the Law depart from your mouth; meditate on it day and night, so that you may be careful to do everything written in it. Then you will be prosperous and successful.

Joshua 1:8

When Your words came, I ate them; they were my joy and my heart's delight, for I bear Your name, O Lord God Almighty.

Jeremiah 15:16

[Jesus] replied, "Blessed rather are those who hear the word of God and obey it."

Luke 11:28

To the Jews who had believed Him, Jesus said, "If you hold to My teaching, you are really My disciples. Then you will know the truth, and the truth will set you free."

John 8:31-32

*The Word of God hidden in the heart
is a stubborn voice to suppress.*
Billy Graham

Dear Father, thank You for Your Word. Thank You for it's guidance and direction and for the reminders of Your work in Your children's lives. It tells me that You love me.

Amen.

Broken Hearts

When someone you care about is hurting, you just want to help, don't you? You may wish with all your heart that you could just fix her problem. Make it go away. Turn back the clock to before the pain began. Of course, no one can do that.

But there is something you can do – pray. Interceding on behalf of someone who is grieving is an important privilege of prayer. It is also obedience to God's command to love one another.

Praying God's comfort and peace into a broken heart shows love and concern for a brother or sister. It also shows a trust in God that He can heal a broken heart, mend the grieving spirit and help this person move past the pain.

Remember to pray for the broken-hearted, not just at the time of loss or pain, but for days and months afterward and whenever God brings her to mind. Pain and grief know no time limits. God is always needed.

Is any one of you in trouble? He should pray. Is anyone happy? Let him sing songs of praise. Is any one of you sick? He should call the elders of the church to pray over him and anoint him with oil in the name of the Lord. And the prayer offered in faith will make the sick person well; the Lord will raise him up. If he has sinned, he will be forgiven.

James 5:13-15

Those who know Your name will trust in You, for You, LORD, have never forsaken those who seek You.

Psalm 9:10

The LORD is righteous in all His ways and loving toward all He has made. The LORD is near to all who call on Him, to all who call on Him in truth.

Psalm 145:17-18

Therefore confess your sins to each other and pray for each other so that you may be healed. The prayer of a righteous man is powerful and effective.

James 5:16

[Praise be to God] who comforts us in all our troubles, so that we can comfort those in any trouble with the comfort we ourselves have received from God.

2 Corinthians 1:4

Very early in the morning, while it was still dark, Jesus got up, left the house and went off to a solitary place, where He prayed.

Mark 1:35

If you seek Him, He will be found by you; but if you forsake Him, He will reject you forever.

1 Chronicles 28:9

Then you will call upon Me and come and pray to Me, and I will listen to you. You will seek Me and find Me when you seek Me with all your heart.

Jeremiah 29:12-13

When you cannot stand,
He will bear you in His arms.
Francis de Sales

Dear Father, thank You for the reminder that You will carry us when we don't have the strength to walk. Thank You Father, for Your love.

Amen.

Praise God's Creativity

Thank God for His amazing creativity. Think about it. How can you hold a newborn baby and not be amazed at the miracle of life. A tiny body that will grow, inside and out, into adulthood but has everything it needs to sustain life, even before entering this world.

Look around at nature. From a colorful butterfly to the humpback whale, God's creativity is evident. Every creature shows the variety of His Creation. The colors on our planet, blue skies, aqua water, green grass, white-capped mountains, flowers in every hue imaginable. He is creative beyond belief.

God knows that different things in nature speak to different hearts. He knew that some people would hear the ocean's roar and think of Him. Some would gaze at the majestic mountains and think of Him.

Others would watch deer frolicking in a meadow and be reminded of God's loving Creation. He made them all and He made them for His children to enjoy. Thank Him for His creativity.

In the beginning God created the heavens and the earth.

Genesis 1:1

By faith we understand that the universe was formed at God's command, so that what is seen was not made out of what was visible.

Hebrews 11:3

For You created my inmost being; You knit me together in my mother's womb. I praise You because I am fearfully and wonderfully made; Your works are wonderful, I know that full well.

Psalm 139:13-14

"I am the LORD, who has made all things, who alone stretched out the heavens, who spread out the earth by Myself."

Isaiah 44:24

Through Him all things were made; without Him nothing was made that has been made.

John 1:3

For us there is but one God, the Father, from whom all things came and for whom we live; and there is but one Lord, Jesus Christ, through whom all things came and through whom we live.

1 Corinthians 8:6

For by Him all things were created: things in heaven and on earth, visible and invisible, whether thrones or powers or rulers or authorities; all things were created by Him and for Him.

Colossians 1:16

One Lord, one faith, one baptism; one God and Father of all, who is over all and through all and in all.

Ephesians 4:5-6

Either God is in the whole of nature,
with no gaps, or He's not there at all.
                              L. A. Coulson

❧

Dear Father, You are so creative. I am constantly amazed at all You've created. So many varieties of colors, animals, people, landscapes. Thank You for sharing Your hard work with us.

                              Amen.

Help My Unbelief

Scripture tells us that without faith it is impossible to please God. Wow, that's kind of scary, isn't it? Faith is believing in what you cannot see – believing God's hand is in all of life.

Believing He is in control, even when you can't see where or how. It isn't easy sometimes. One man in Scripture very honestly cried out to Jesus, "I do believe. Help Thou my unbelief." We never believe as much as we could. There is always room for faith to grow.

Some things are easy to accept about God. Others are more difficult. When you can't see His hand in a situation and when you don't have a clue about His plan for the future, faith comes a little more slowly.

Pray for God to strengthen your faith muscle. Join the man in Scripture who prayed, "I do believe. Help thou my unbelief."

Now faith is being sure of what we hope for and certain of what we do not see.

Hebrews 11:1

"I tell you the truth, whoever hears My word and believes Him who sent Me has eternal life and will not be condemned; he has crossed over from death to life."

John 5:24

I am not ashamed, because I know whom I have believed, and am convinced that He is able to guard what I have entrusted to Him for that day.

2 Timothy 1:12

However, to the man who does not work but trusts God who justifies the wicked, his faith is credited as righteousness.

Romans 4:5

"Everything is possible for him who believes."

Mark 9:23

Show me your faith without deeds, and I will show you my faith by what I do.

James 2:18

Love the LORD, all His saints! The LORD preserves the faithful, but the proud He pays back in full. Be strong and take heart, all you who hope in the LORD.

Psalm 31:23-24

For it is by grace you have been saved, through faith – and this not from yourselves, it is the gift of God – not by works, so that no one can boast.

Ephesians 2:8-9

One person with a belief is equal to a force of 99 who only have interests.

Anonymous

Dear Father, sometimes I can believe so easily and then, sometimes it's so hard. Father, help me to believe and trust. How can I love if I don't trust? Please help me.

Amen.

Thank You for Forgiveness

How good are you at forgiving someone who hurts you? Do you live by the adage, "I'll forgive but I won't forget." Here's a news flash, if you don't forget, you haven't truly forgiven. Whatever you refuse to forget is still on the ledger against the person you say you've forgiven.

Everyone needs forgiveness once in a while. Forgiveness becomes a reciprocal thing. Everyone constantly needs forgiveness from God. No reciprocity there – He never needs it.

Even so, God is our model for forgiveness. He forgives and forgets. He says that our sins – the disobedience that hurts Him so much – are cast away "as far as the East is from the West."

What a model for us to forgive *and* forget. Thank God for His forgiveness and ask Him for help in modeling complete forgiveness yourself.

"Though your sins are like scarlet, they shall be as white as snow; though they are red as crimson, they shall be like wool."

Isaiah 1:18

If we confess our sins, He is faithful and just and will forgive us our sins and purify us from all unrighteousness.

1 John 1:9

Be kind and compassionate to one another, forgiving each other, just as in Christ God forgave you.

Ephesians 4:32

Bear with each other and forgive whatever grievances you may have against one another. Forgive as the Lord forgave you.

Colossians 3:13

"Forgive us our debts, as we also have forgiven our debtors."

Matthew 6:12

But with You there is forgiveness; therefore You are feared.

Psalm 130:4

They refused to listen and failed to remember the miracles You performed among them. They became stiff-necked and in their rebellion appointed a leader in order to return to their slavery. But You are a forgiving God, gracious and compassionate, slow to anger and abounding in love.

Nehemiah 9:17

All the prophets testify about Him that everyone who believes in Him receives forgiveness of sins through His name.

Acts 10:43

God has cast our confessed sin into the depths of the sea, and He's even put a "No Fishing" sign over the spot.

Dwight L. Moody

Dear Father, I'm so thankful for forgiveness because I know I don't deserve it. Help me to model Your forgiveness to others.

Amen.

Pray for Growth

It's such a joy to watch a young child grow and mature. You see the joy in the face of a baby when he takes his first steps; the thrill of accomplishment in a child who is learning to read; the pride of a young athlete who masters new skills; the excitement of a teenager learning to drive. Growth and development are rewarding and encouraging!

What about spiritual growth? It's harder to measure and more fluid as lessons are learned, then forgotten, then relearned again. Support your loved ones with prayers for their spiritual growth. Ask God to teach them about faith and to gently take them along the path to maturity with Him.

Encourage your loved ones not to get discouraged in this journey. Some lessons are hard to learn, but the rewards of growing closer to God are immeasurable and amazing. Ask God for spiritual growth.

Then we will no longer be infants, tossed back and forth by the waves, and blown here and there by every wind of teaching and by the cunning and craftiness of men in their deceitful scheming. Instead, speaking the truth in love, we will in all things grow up into Him who is the Head, that is, Christ.

Ephesians 4:14-15

Acknowledge the God of your father, and serve Him with wholehearted devotion and with a willing mind, for the LORD searches every heart and understands every motive behind the thoughts. If you seek Him, He will be found by you; but if you forsake Him, He will reject you forever.

1 Chronicles 28:9

Grow in the grace and knowledge of our Lord and Savior Jesus Christ.

2 Peter 3:18

We, who with unveiled faces all reflect the Lord's glory, are being transformed into His likeness with ever-increasing glory, which comes from the Lord, who is the Spirit.

2 Corinthians 3:18

Like newborn babies, crave pure spiritual milk, so that by it you may grow up in your salvation, now that you have tasted that the Lord is good.

I Peter 2:2-3

Do your best to present yourself to God as one approved, a workman who does not need to be ashamed and who correctly handles the word of truth.

2 Timothy 2:15

Being confident of this, that He who began a good work in you will carry it on to completion until the day of Christ Jesus.

Philippians 1:6

We pray this in order that you may live a life worthy of the Lord and may please Him in every way: bearing fruit in every good work, growing in the knowledge of God, being strengthened with all power according to His glorious might so that you may have great endurance and patience, and joyfully giving thanks to the Father, who has qualified you to share in the inheritance of the saints in the kingdom of light.

Colossians 1:10-12

Prayer involves transformed passions.
In prayer, real prayer, we begin to think
God's thoughts after Him: to desire the
things He desires: to love the things He
loves: to will the things He wills.

Richard J. Foster

Dear Father, I long to know You better, to
grow deeper in my faith. I long to be of service to You. Father, help me to trust, grow
and serve.

Amen.

Thank God for
the Privilege of Prayer

Prayer may well be the least understood of all privileges afforded to believers. Are you truly able to change God's mind when you pray for things? Does the God of the universe listen to what you have to say and how you feel? Does He have time to care about little old you?

The simple answer to all of those questions is ... Yes. Actually, it is, "Yes, but ... " You knew there would be a catch, right? Well, the catch is only that you must be in tune with Him. Then you will be desiring what He wants and praying in that direction.

Think about what a privilege it is to be able to come before God, the Creator, with your requests and concerns. He wants to hear what's on your heart. He wants to know what concerns you. He wants to know you trust Him enough to ask for His intervention and help.

"When you pray, go into your room, close the door and pray to your Father, who is unseen. Then your Father, who sees what is done in secret, will reward you."

Matthew 6:6

"Before they call I will answer; while they are still speaking I will hear."

Isaiah 65:24

"If you believe, you will receive whatever you ask for in prayer."

Matthew 21:22

"If you remain in Me and My words remain in you, ask whatever you wish, and it will be given you."

John 15:7

He will call upon Me, and I will answer him; I will be with him in trouble, I will deliver him and honor him.

Psalm 91:15

Let us then approach the throne of grace with confidence, so that we may receive mercy and find grace to help us in our time of need.

Hebrews 4:16

I call on You, O God, for You will answer me; give ear to me and hear my prayer.

Psalm 17:6

"We know that God does not listen to sinners. He listens to the godly man who does His will."

John 9:31

There is not in the world a kind of life more sweet and delightful than that of a continual conversation with God.

Brother Lawrence

Dear Father, I'm so grateful for the privilege of being able to talk with You whenever I want. Thank You for hearing my prayers and caring about the things that are on my heart.

Amen.

Praise God's Power

Theologians will tell you that there is constantly a battle being fought in the spiritual realm. The object of the battle – the prize being fought over – is you.

Sometimes you may be aware of the struggle for your allegiance and love. Particularly following a spiritual high you may notice that life is suddenly harder and more painful. Satan is trying to grab you back. He is powerful. He is sneaky and he never has your best interests in mind. He only wants to take from God and if you are God's child he will try to pull you away from your Father.

The good news ... the reason to praise is that God is more powerful than Satan. He will always and forever win. Satan has no chance against God. And he has no chance against you if you call on God's power to fight for you.

Ask God to protect you from Satan's arrows and to help you stand strong by putting on the armor He provides for you.

Who shall separate us from the love of Christ? Shall trouble or hardship or persecution or famine or nakedness or danger or sword? No, in all these things we are more than conquerors through Him who loved us.

Romans 8:35, 37

For the eyes of the LORD range throughout the earth to strengthen those whose hearts are fully committed to Him.

2 Chronicles 16:9

So we say with confidence, "The Lord is my Helper; I will not be afraid. What can man do to me?"

Hebrews 13:6

The LORD is my strength and my shield; my heart trusts in Him, and I am helped. My heart leaps for joy and I will give thanks to Him in song.

Psalm 28:7

Finally, be strong in the Lord and in His mighty power. Put on the full armor of God so that you can take your stand against the devil's schemes.

Ephesians 6:10-11

Let us be self-controlled, putting on faith and love as a breastplate, and the hope of salvation as a helmet.

1 Thessalonians 5:8

The voice of the LORD is powerful; the voice of the LORD is majestic.

Psalm 29:4

If we are thrown into the blazing furnace, the God we serve is able to save us from it, and He will rescue us from your hand, O king.

Daniel 3:17

Have courage for the great sorrows
of life and patience for the small ones.
And when you have finished
your daily task, go to sleep
in peace. God is awake.

Victor Hugo

Dear Father, what would I do if Your power
wasn't available to me. Thank You for sup-
plying me with power. Thank You for guiding
and directing my life.

Amen.

Redeem the Time

There was once a Bible college professor who began his early morning class times by challenging his students to "Redeem the time." What does that mean?

He was reminding his students that each person is given a certain number of days to live on this earth. Of course, no one knows what that number is. So, make your days count. Live with focus.

God has given you life for a reason – to glorify Him, to live for Him, to share the message of His love with others. Each person lives out this purpose in different ways. What it means for you is between you and God. But once you understand that purpose, don't lose sight of it.

Redeeming the time means you aren't lazily wasting your days watching television or strolling through shopping malls.

Redeeming-the-time-living looks at every new day as a fresh opportunity to serve God intentionally. Pray for an understanding of how you can "redeem the time".

"Let your light shine before men, that they may see your good deeds and praise your Father in heaven."

Matthew 5:16

For we are God's workmanship, created in Christ Jesus to do good works, which God prepared in advance for us to do.

Ephesians 2:10

"No one can serve two masters. Either he will hate the one and love the other, or he will be devoted to the one and despise the other. You cannot serve both God and Money."

Matthew 6:24

"You will receive power when the Holy Spirit comes on you; and you will be My witnesses in Jerusalem, and in all Judea and Samaria, and to the ends of the earth."

Acts 1:8

Therefore, I urge you, brothers, in view of God's mercy, to offer your bodies as living sacrifices, holy and pleasing to God – this is your spiritual act of worship. Do not conform any longer to the pattern of this world, but be transformed by the renewing of your mind. Then you will be able to test and approve what God's will is – His good, pleasing and perfect will.

Romans 12:1-2

It is the Lord your God you must follow, and Him you must revere. Keep His commands and obey Him; serve Him and hold fast to Him.

Deuteronomy 13:4

This is how we know what love is: Jesus Christ laid down His life for us. And we ought to lay down our lives for our brothers. If anyone has material possessions and sees his brother in need but has no pity on him, how can the love of God be in him? Dear children, let us not love with words or tongue but with actions and in truth.

1 John 3:16-18

God has created me to do Him some definite service; He has committed some work to me which He has not committed to another. I have my mission. I may never know it in this life, but I shall be told it in the next.

John Henry Newman

Dear Father, show me how to redeem the time and make my days count for You. Father, use me in Your service.

Amen.